Get set... GO!

Pluck and Scrape

Sally Hewitt

Photography by Peter Millard

Contents

CHILDRENS PRESS®
CHICAGO

Introduction

Sound waves are made when air vibrates.
This means the air moves back and forth
very, very, fast.
You cannot see sound waves,
but you can hear them.

We play stringed instruments by
plucking the strings with our fingers
or scraping them with a bow.
The strings vibrate
and move the air around them.
A musical note is heard.

All the instruments in the picture
are sound boxes with air inside.
When the air in the instrument vibrates,
it makes a loud sound.

Get ready to make some instruments
to pluck and scrape.

Violin

Viola

Cello

bow

bow

Guitar

Rubber band

Get ready

✔ Rubber band   ✔ Your fingers

. . . Get Set

Stretch the rubber band
between your thumb and first finger.

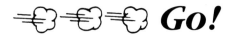 **Go!**

Pluck the rubber band with
the first finger of your other hand.
The rubber band vibrates and plays a note.
Pull your fingers apart
to stretch the band tighter.
It plays a higher note.
Put your fingers closer together
to loosen the band.
It plays a lower note.

Sound boxes

Get ready

✔ Rubber bands of different sizes

✔ Small boxes, plastic cups, jars

. . . Get Set

Stretch rubber bands around the containers.

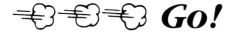 **_Go!_**

Pluck the part of the rubber band that is stretched over the opening of each container.
The moving rubber band vibrates the air inside the container and makes a loud sound.
Containers make good sound boxes.

Tissue box guitar

Get ready

✔ Empty tissue box
✔ Strong cardboard

✔ 4 long rubber bands, all the same size

. . . Get Set

Ask an adult to cut the cardboard into
a triangle shape to make
a bridge like this:
Make sure it is long enough
to fit across your box.
Stretch the rubber bands around the box.
Slide the bridge underneath them
and stand it up.

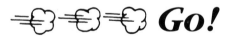 **_Go!_**

Pluck the strings and listen.
You can make more guitars
with different-sized boxes.

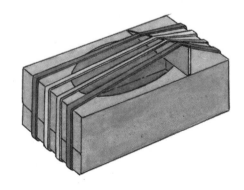

Tight and loose

Get ready

✔ Strong cardboard box ✔ Long piece of string
✔ Pencil

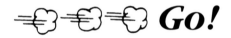

. . . Get Set

Tie the string around the box.
Push the pencil between the string
and the box at one end.

Go!

Pluck the string and listen.
Twist the pencil around
to tighten the string.
Pluck it and listen again.
Now the note will sound higher.
The tighter the string,
the higher the note it plays.

Double bass

Get ready

✔ Long stick
   (dowel rod or
   bamboo stick)

✔ Large cardboard box
✔ Button
✔ Long piece of string

. . . Get Set

Tie the button to one end of the string.
Ask an adult to make two holes
in opposite corners of the box.
One is for the string and one is for the stick.
Thread the string through from the inside
of the box.
Push the stick down through the other hole.
Stretch the string tightly.
Tie the end to the top of the stick.

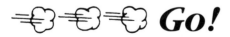 **_Go!_**

Move the stick back and forth as you
pluck the string to make different notes.

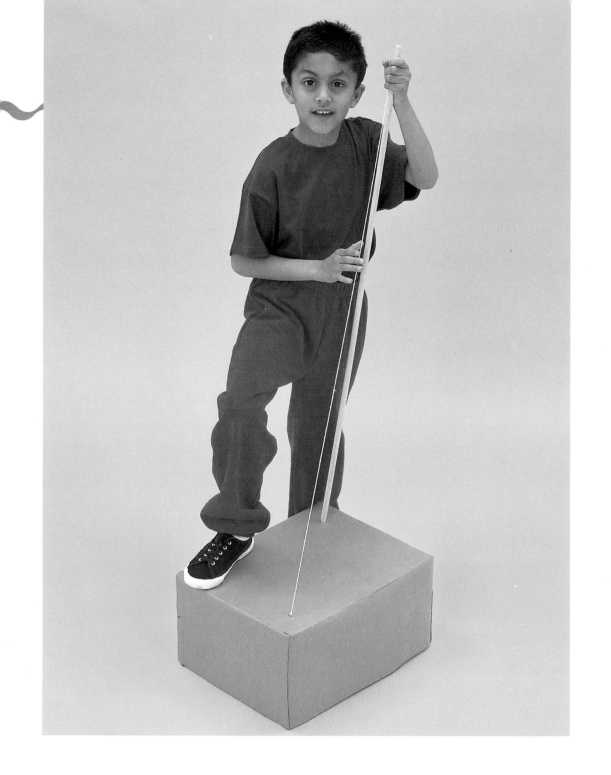

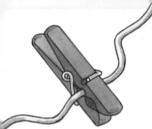

Bottle bass

Get ready

- ✔ Plastic bottle
- ✔ Dowel rod (twice as long as the bottle)
- ✔ Long piece of string
- ✔ Modeling clay
- ✔ Snap clothespin

. . . Get Set

Ask an adult to make one hole in the bottom of the bottle, and one hole near the bottom. Thread the string through the holes and tie it. Push the dowel rod into the bottle. Stretch the string tightly and tie the end to the top of the rod. Clip the clothespin to the string. Stick its base to the side of the bottle with modeling clay to tighten the string.

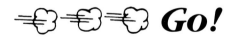 **Go!**

Pluck the string and listen.

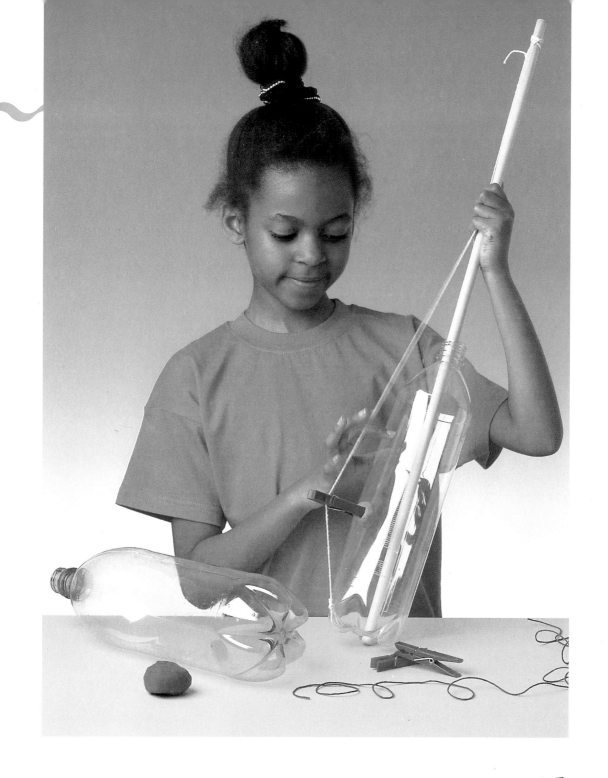

Rubber band harp

Get ready

✔ Styrofoam box

✔ Paper fasteners

✔ Rubber bands of different lengths

. . . Get Set

Press the paper fasteners into the styrofoam box
in pairs, different distances apart.
Be careful not to push them all the way in.
Stretch a rubber band over the ends of
each pair of fasteners.

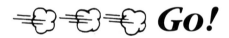 Go!

Pluck each one and listen to the sound it makes.
The shorter rubber bands make higher sounds
than the longer ones.

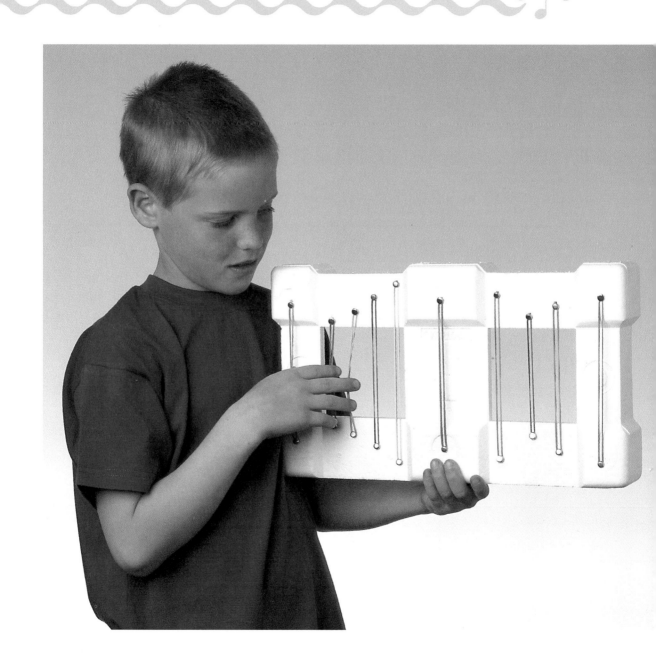

Twanger

Get ready

✔ Chopstick or
wooden ruler

✔ Table

. . . Get Set

Hold one end of the chopstick or ruler
down on the edge of the table.
Let the other end stick out
over the table edge.

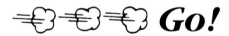 **Go!**

Use your other hand to "twang"
the end of the chopstick or ruler.
Listen.
The table acts as a very large sound board
which helps you make the sound louder.
Can you feel the vibrations?

Scrapers

Get ready

- ✔ Your double bass or your bottle bass
- ✔ Pencil
- ✔ Stick
- ✔ Strip of corrugated cardboard

. . . Get Set

Pull the bass string tight.

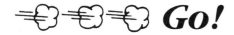 **Go!**

Run the stick, the cardboard,
and the pencil over the string
as if they were bows.
Listen to the sounds they make.
The rough stick and the cardboard
vibrate the string.
The smooth pencil hardly vibrates it at all.

Make a bow

Get ready

✔ Plastic coat hanger
   with hooks (as shown)

✔ Your instruments
✔ String or shoelace

. . . Get Set

Tie the string or shoelace tightly to
each end of the coat hanger
to make a bow.

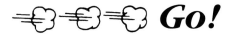 **Go!**

Scrape the strings of your instruments
with your bow.
What kinds of sounds
do they make?

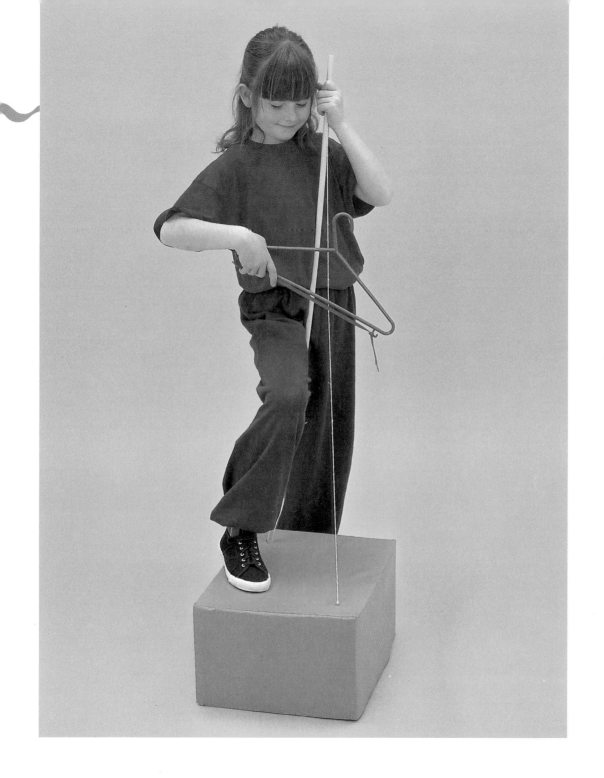

Index

Acknowledgments: The author and publisher would like to thank the pupils of Kenmont Primary School, London, for their participation in the photographs of this book.

Editor: Pippa Pollard
Design: Ruth Levy
Cover design: Mike Davis
Artwork: Ruth Levy

Library of Congress Cataloging-in-Publication Data

Hewitt, Sally.
  Pluck and scrape / by Sally Hewitt.
    p.   cm. — (Get set— go!)
  Includes index.
  ISBN 0-516-07991-3
    1. Musical instruments—Construction—Juvenile literature.
  [1. Musical instruments—Construction.] I. Series.
  ML460.H48   1994
  787'.19—dc20   94-16939
                                                    CIP
                                                    AC

1994 Childrens Press® Edition
© 1993 Watts Books, London, New York, Sydney
All rights reserved. Printed in the United States of America.
Published simultaneously in Canada.
1 2 3 4 5 6 7 8 9 0 R 03 02 01 00 99 98 97 96 95 94